SCIENCE
AN IMAGINATION LIBRARY SERIES

Ghosts

by Jacqueline Laks Gorman

Gareth Stevens Publishing
A WORLD ALMANAC EDUCATION GROUP COMPANY

Please visit our web site at: www.garethstevens.com
For a free color catalog describing Gareth Stevens Publishing's
list of high-quality books and multimedia programs,
call 1-800-542-2595 (USA) or 1-800-387-3178 (Canada).
Gareth Stevens Publishing's fax: (414) 332-3567.

Library of Congress Cataloging-in-Publication Data

Gorman, Jacqueline Laks, 1955-
    Ghosts / by Jacqueline Laks Gorman.
        p. cm. — (X science: an imagination library series)
    Includes bibliographical references and index.
    Summary: Introduces ghosts, describing what people believe about them and examples
of sightings of different ghosts.
    ISBN 0-8368-3199-3 (lib. bdg.)
    1. Ghosts—Juvenile literature. [1. Ghosts.] I. Title. II. Series.
    BF1461.G67   2002
    133.1—dc21   2002022526

First published in 2002 by
Gareth Stevens Publishing
A World Almanac Education Group Company
330 West Olive Street, Suite 100
Milwaukee, WI 53212 USA

Text: Jacqueline Laks Gorman
Cover design and page layout: Tammy Gruenewald
Series editor: Betsy Rasmussen
Picture Researcher: Diane Laska-Swanke

Photo credits: Cover © Derek Stafford/Fortean Picture Library; p. 5 © Fortean Picture Library;
p. 7 Jude Huff-Felz, Courtesy of Ghost Research Society; p. 9 © Bettmann/CORBIS; pp. 11, 21
Photofest; p. 13 © Mary Evans Picture Library; pp. 15 (both), 17 (inset) © North Wind Picture
Archives; p. 17 (main) © Stephen G. St. John/NGS Image Collection; p. 19 © Janet & Colin
Bord/Fortean Picture Library

Printed in the United States of America

1 2 3 4 5 6 7 8 9 06 05 04 03 02

Front cover: A dark figure called the "Black Abbot"
can be seen in a churchyard near Cheltenham, England.
Is it the ghost of a man who haunts the church?

TABLE OF CONTENTS

Words that appear in the glossary are printed in **boldface**
type the first time they occur in the text.

ARE THERE GHOSTS?

Have you ever heard strange noises late at night? Have you ever seen flickering lights in the dark? Have you ever been in a room alone and felt that something — or someone — was there with you?

Maybe it was a ghost.

For thousands of years, people have told stories about ghosts, **haunted** houses, and other haunted places. Sometimes the ghostly happenings in these tales can be explained. Sometimes, though, they cannot. Maybe the spirits of the dead are here on Earth after all.

A woman in Australia took a photograph of her daughter's grave. The woman said the picture showed a young child that she had never seen before. Could the child be a ghost?

SPIRITS WHO WANT TO STAY

Ghosts are the spirits of people who have died, but instead of leaving the world, they continue to visit the living. Maybe the person died suddenly, and the spirit wants to finish things that never got done. Maybe the spirit is sorry for bad things the person did before dying. Maybe the spirit has messages for others. Or maybe the spirit just wants to stay in the place where the person was happy.

While some ghosts reportedly play tricks on people, most do not seem to want to hurt anyone. Really, ghosts do not seem to pay any attention to people at all. They just act out a scene over and over again.

A group of ghost researchers visited Bachelor's Grove Cemetery in Chicago in 1991. They took this picture. It seems to show the ghost of a woman wearing an old-fashioned dress and sitting on a tombstone.

GHOST SHIPS AND TRAINS

Not all ghosts are spirits of people. Reports have been made of **phantom** ships that are seen sailing the seas long after they have sunk. The most famous phantom ship is the *Flying Dutchman*. The *Flying Dutchman* left Holland in 1680 and sank in a bad storm. Everyone aboard died. Over the years, hundreds of people have reported seeing the *Flying Dutchman*. Some sailors think the ghost ship appears when danger is coming.

Some people claim they have seen phantom cars and trains. According to some reports, the entire car or train appears. According to others, the lights appear. Observers say the car or train travels along its original route but never reaches its final stop.

In April 1865, a funeral train carried the body of Abraham Lincoln from Washington, DC to Illinois. Some people say they have seen the ghost of the funeral train traveling the same tracks every year on the date of Lincoln's death.

POLTERGEISTS

Poltergeists are a special type of ghost. These ghosts are noisy and mean, and they do bad things. Poltergeists shake furniture, break dishes, set fires, and throw people and things around.

It seems that in many cases, a poltergeist haunts teenagers. Sometimes, however, the teenager is doing the strange things on purpose to get attention or just to play a joke on someone.

Some researchers, though, think these teenagers are really not doing anything. The teen may be very upset. The researchers believe these strong emotions may somehow create a type of **energy**, or **force**, that makes the strange things happen.

This shot is from the movie *Poltergeist* (1982). It shows children floating in the air after being raised up by the poltergeist. No one knows for sure what, or who, is responsible for all the pranks that happen.

SPIRITUALISM

Spiritualism is the belief that some people can communicate with the dead. This communication comes through mediums — people who say they can talk to spirits.

A spiritualism **craze** happened in the United States in 1848. Two young sisters, Maggie and Katie Fox, said they were getting messages from a dead man who made secret knocking sounds. Maggie and Katie became famous and toured the country.

In 1888, the Fox sisters admitted they had been pretending. The sisters made the knocking sounds by cracking their toes. Even so, many people still believed in spiritualism, and other mediums became popular, too.

In 1909, a Polish medium named Stanislawa Tomczyk demonstrated her ability to raise objects using her mental powers. There may be real mediums who have special **psychic** powers, but many mediums are fakes.

THE HAUNTED WHITE HOUSE

The White House is not just the home of the president. Some people believe that several ghosts live there, too. Abraham Lincoln's ghost, for example, has been seen walking in the halls and looking out a window of the **Oval Office**. People staying in the Lincoln Bedroom at the White House say they have seen him come in, sit on the bed, and take off his boots.

President Andrew Jackson has been seen laughing in his bedroom. President William Henry Harrison has been heard in the attic. Abigail Adams, who was the first lady many years ago, has been seen in the East Room — hanging up laundry!

First Lady Abigail Adams (*left*) and President Andrew Jackson (*right*) are just two of the famous ghosts who are said to haunt the White House.

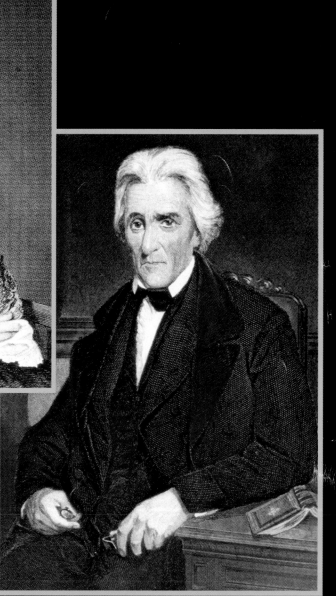

THE GHOSTS OF OCTAGON HOUSE

The **Octagon** House in Washington, DC, is reported to have many ghosts. John Tayloe, the first owner of the house, had a fight with his daughter one night. The daughter fell down the stairs and died. Years later, Tayloe had another fight with a different daughter on the same stairs. This daughter also fell and died. Reports say that a ghostly candle can sometimes be seen on the stairs, followed by the sounds of a scream and something falling.

The Octagon House was a stop on the **Underground Railroad**, too. Ghosts of runaway slaves and **Civil War** soldiers are said to haunt this house. Also, people smell food cooking in the kitchen and hear strange sounds.

The Octagon House is now a museum. After the White House was burned by the British in 1814, President James Madison lived at Octagon House with his wife, Dolley (inset photo). Dolley's ghost is often heard there, meeting her guests.

Inset: © North Wind Picture Archives

EXPLAINING GHOSTLY SIGHTS AND SOUNDS

Are ghosts real, or are people just imagining them? Situations can seem strange at night, which is when most people say they see ghosts. Perhaps the people who see ghosts are only half awake and still dreaming.

Some reported ghost sightings are fakes. It is not hard to make ghostly noises and play ghostly tricks.

Many ghostly sights and sounds can be explained in other ways. For instance, heating pipes can make knocking sounds. Car lights outside can reflect and cause moving lights inside. Ghostly footsteps might really be floorboards that shrink as the temperature cools. Scratching sounds might be birds on the roof or mice in the walls.

This picture looks like it shows a ghost, but it is just a fake. Some photos that are supposed to show ghosts are really just **double exposures**.

POPULAR GHOSTS

People love ghosts and ghost stories even if they do not believe in them. Many great authors have written ghost stories. One famous ghost story is *A Christmas Carol*, by Charles Dickens. In this story, a ghost visits his friend, Ebenezer Scrooge, in order to help Scrooge become a better person. This tale has also been made into movies and plays.

Many people like to watch movies about ghosts. Some of the movies are scary, but others are funny. It seems everyone likes to tell, or hear, a ghost story.

In the 1995 movie *Casper*, the **title character** is the friendly ghost of a young boy. These three ghosts are Casper's uncles, and they hate people.

MORE TO READ AND VIEW

Books (Nonfiction)   *Haunting of America: Ghost Stories from Our Past.* Jean Anderson (Houghton Mifflin)
Headless Haunt and Other African-American Ghost Stories. James S. Haskins (Harper Collins)
Scary Science: The Truth Behind Vampires, Witches, UFOs, Ghosts and More! Sylvia Funston (Owl Books)

Books (Fiction)   *Case of the Haunted Camp.* Nina Alexander (Scholastic)
Christmas Carol. Charles Dickens and Lisbeth Zwerger (North South Books)
Cold Feet. Cynthia Defelice (DK Publishing)
Dial-A-Ghost. Eva Ibbotson (Dutton Books)
Ghosts Don't Eat Potato Chips. Adventures of the Bailey School Kids. (series). Debbie Dadey and Marcia Thornton Jones (Little Apple)
Ghosts! Ghostly Tales from Folklore. Alvin Schwartz (HarperTrophy)
I Dare You: Stories to Scare You. Kathleen Keeler and Bob Doucet (Cartwheel Books)
Lucy Dove. Janice Del Negro (DK Publishing)
Old Devil Wind. Bill Martin, Jr. (Harcourt Brace & Company)

Videos (Nonfiction)   *Secrets of the Unknown: English Ghosts.* (MPI Home Videos)
The Unexplained: Hauntings. (A&E series)
The Unexplained: Poltergeist. (A&E series)

Videos (Fiction)   *Casper.* (Universal Studios)
Casper Meets Wendy. (Twentieth Century Fox)
The Muppet Christmas Carol. (Jim Henson Video)

WEB SITES

Web sites change frequently, but we believe the following web sites are going to last. You can also use good search engines, such as **Yahooligans! [www.yahooligans.com]** or **Google [www.google.com]** to find more information about ghosts. Some keywords that will help you are: *ghosts, poltergeist, spiritualism, haunted houses, phantoms,* and *graveyards.*

www.ajkids.com

Ask Jeeves Kids, the junior Ask Jeeves site, is a great place to do research. Try asking:

Are ghosts real?

What do ghosts do?

You can also just type in words and phrases with "?" at the end, such as:

Spirit world?

Haunted houses?

www.yahooligans.com

This junior version of the Yahoo site is very easy to use. Simply type in the word "ghost" or "ghosts" to get a list of sites that are appropriate for kids.

www.americanfolklore.net

American Folklore retells folklore, myths, legends, tall tales, and ghost stories from each of the fifty states.

www.graveyards.com/bachelors

Visit this site to learn all about *Bachelor's Grove Cemetery* in Chicago — a very haunted place!

www.nationalgeographic.com/castles

Poke around the rooms of a stone castle and learn about the ghosts that haunt there, at this *National Geographic* site.

www.discovery.com/stories/history/pirates/ pirates.html

This *Pirate Ghosts* site introduces you to some of the most feared pirates of all time. They are said to be coming back to life, because divers are disturbing the wreckage of their ships.

www.historychannel.com/exhibits/halloween

Discover facts about Halloween, ghost stories, Jack-o-lanterns, and more at this *History Channel* site.

GLOSSARY

You can find these words on the pages listed. Reading a word in a sentence helps you understand it even better.

Civil War (SIV-uhl WOHR) — a war that took place between two groups within the United States. 16

craze (KRAYZ) — something people become excited, or crazy, about for a time. 12

double exposures (DUH-buhl ek-SPOH-shurz) — when two images appear on the same piece of film. 18

energy (EN-urr-gee) — power. 10

force (FOHRS) — a motion or a change. 10

haunted (HAWNT-ehd) — visited or inhabited by a ghost. 4, 10, 14, 16

octagon (AHK-tuh-gon) — an eight-sided shape. 16

Oval Office (OH-vuhl OFF-iss) — the president's private office in the White House. 14

phantom (FAN-tuhm) — a ghost. 8

psychic (SYE-kik) — someone sensitive to spiritual forces or who understands spirits. 12

title character (TY-til KHAYR-ak-tur) — the person or other being in a story after which the story is named. 20

Underground Railroad (UHN-der-grownd RAYL-rohd) — a network used to help slaves escape to freedom before 1863. 16

INDEX